WILDE EDIBLE PLANTS FORAGE

Discovering Nature's Bounty of edible plants
in North America

BY

Lomasi Harvest

TABLE OF CONTENT

INTRODUCTION

Welcome to the captivating world of wild edible plants—an exploration of nature's bounty that offers sustenance and a deeper connection with the earth. Foraging for wild edibles involves identifying, harvesting, and utilizing plants growing in the wild, providing a rich tapestry of flavours, nutrition, and cultural heritage. In this journey, we embark on a discovery of common wild edible plants, understanding their characteristics, and learning how to differentiate them from potentially harmful flora.

Venturing into the realm of wild edibles requires a blend of knowledge, caution, and respect for nature. This endeavour not only offers the opportunity to enrich our diets with diverse and nutrient-rich foods but also fosters a sense of reverence for the environment. Let us delve into this captivating adventure, appreciating the beauty and benefits that wild edible plants bring to our lives while ensuring safety and sustainability in our foraging practices.

CHAPTER ONE
Understanding Wild Edible Plants

Certainly! "Understanding Wild Edible Plants" is a crucial section of a guide on wild edible plant foraging. In this section, readers will gain foundational knowledge about what wild edible plants are their significance, characteristics, and considerations for identifying and safely consuming them.

1. Definition and Significance

- **Definition**: Wild edible plants refer to plants found in their natural habitat that are safe for human consumption. These plants have a history of being utilized for food by various cultures throughout history.

- **Significance**: Understanding wild edible plants is essential for survival skills, sustainable living, connecting with nature, and enriching one's diet with diverse and nutritious foods.

2. Characteristics of Wild Edible Plants

- **Diversity**: Wild edible plants encompass a wide range of species, including various greens, fruits, nuts, roots, and more.

- **Adaptability**: These plants are adapted to their specific environments and have developed unique features to thrive in diverse habitats.

- **Seasonality**: Wild edibles often have distinct growing seasons, and their availability may vary based on climate, region, and local conditions.

- **Nutritional Value**: Wild edible plants can be highly nutritious, providing essential vitamins, minerals, antioxidants, and dietary fibre.

3. Basic Botanical Knowledge

- **Plant Parts**: Understanding the different parts of a plant, such as leaves, stems, flowers, fruits, and roots, is crucial for identifying edible portions.

- **Plant Families**: Learning about plant families can aid in identifying related edible plants and understanding their characteristics.

4. Toxicity and Potential Hazards

- **Poisonous Plants**: Awareness of poisonous plants is vital to prevent accidental ingestion and ensure safety during foraging.

- **Look-Alikes**: Some edible plants may resemble toxic ones, emphasizing the need for accurate identification to avoid confusion.

5. Cautions and Considerations

- **Allergies**: Some wild edible plants may trigger allergic reactions in individuals with specific sensitivities. Knowing common allergenic plants is important.

- **Medical Conditions**: People with certain medical conditions or taking medications should exercise caution and seek advice before consuming wild plants.

6. Learning Resources and Education

- **Field Guides**: Recommending reliable field guides and books on wild edible plants to aid in identification and learning about their uses.

- **Courses and Workshops**: Encouraging participation in workshops, foraging courses, and guided nature walks to enhance knowledge and practical skills.

7. Cultural and Historical Context

- **Indigenous Knowledge**: Acknowledging the rich tradition and expertise of indigenous cultures in identifying, using, and respecting wild edible plants.

- **Historical Use**: Understanding the historical significance of wild edible plants in human diets and their role in traditional cuisines.

By delving into these aspects, readers will establish a solid foundation for their journey into the fascinating world of wild edible plants, preparing them to responsibly forage and integrate these valuable resources into their lives.

Benefits of Wild Edible Plant Foraging

Wild edible plant foraging offers a plethora of benefits that extend beyond just obtaining food. Here is an exploration of the various advantages:

1. Sustainable and Local Food Source:

- Foraging wild edible plants promotes sustainability by utilizing naturally occurring resources without contributing to commercial agriculture's environmental impact.

- Reduces dependence on mass-produced food and supports local ecosystems.

2. Nutrition and Health:

- Wild edible plants are often nutrient-dense, providing essential vitamins, minerals, antioxidants, and dietary fibre.

- Consuming a diverse range of wild edibles can contribute to a well-rounded and nutritionally rich diet.

3. Connectivity with Nature:

- Foraging encourages a deep connection with the natural environment, fostering a greater appreciation for the biodiversity of plants, their habitats, and ecosystems.

- Promotes outdoor activity and physical exercise, enhancing mental and emotional well-being.

4. Culinary Exploration and Creativity:

- Experimenting with wild edible plants in recipes encourages culinary creativity and a deeper understanding of flavours, textures, and cooking techniques.

- Adds diversity and unique tastes to meals, expanding the palate and cultural culinary experiences.

5. Cost-Effective and Accessible:

- Wild edible plants are often free and readily available in natural environments, reducing grocery costs and making fresh, organic produce accessible to all.

- Foraging can be particularly beneficial for those with limited financial resources.

6. Self-Sufficiency and Survival Skills:

- Learning to identify, harvest, and utilize wild edibles enhances self-sufficiency and survival skills, especially in outdoor or emergency situations.

- Knowledge of edible plants increases self-reliance and confidence in navigating and surviving in the wild.

7. Environmental Stewardship:

- Responsible foraging practices, such as sustainable harvesting and ethical gathering, encourage a sense of environmental responsibility and conservation.

- Raises awareness of the delicate balance between humans and nature, promoting conservation efforts.

8. Education and Cultural Heritage:

- Foraging provides an educational platform to learn about traditional uses of plants by various cultures and indigenous communities.

- Preserves and passes on cultural knowledge and heritage related to wild edibles and sustainable foraging practices.

9. Community and Sharing:

- Foraging can be a communal activity, fostering social connections and opportunities to share knowledge and experiences with others.

- Engages individuals in local community initiatives and events related to foraging, gardening, and sustainability.

10. Resilience and Adaptability:

- Learning to identify and utilize a variety of wild edible plants enhances adaptability, promoting resilience in changing environmental and socio-economic conditions.

By recognizing and embracing these benefits, individuals can fully appreciate the value of wild edible plant foraging, incorporating it into their lifestyle for a more sustainable, nutritious, and connected existence with nature.

Responsible foraging and sustainability

Responsible foraging and sustainability are critical aspects of wild edible plant harvesting that emphasize ethical and environmentally conscious practices. Let us delve into a detailed explanation of both concepts:

Responsible Foraging:

1. **Selective Harvesting:**

- Responsible foragers practice selective harvesting, taking only a portion of a plant without harming its ability to regenerate or reproduce.

- Avoid overharvesting and target invasive or abundant species to maintain a healthy population.

2. **Proper Timing:**

- Harvest plants at the right stage of growth to ensure their optimal flavour, nutrition, and sustainability.

- Avoid harvesting during critical growth periods like flowering or seeding, as this can hinder the plant's ability to reproduce.

3. **Avoidance of Endangered Species:**

- Educated foragers avoid harvesting endangered or threatened plant species to protect their populations and contribute to their conservation.

- Utilize field guides and local resources to identify plants at risk and prioritize their preservation.

4. **Leave No Trace:**

- Adhere to the "Leave No Trace" principles, ensuring minimal impact on the environment during foraging.

- Dispose of waste properly, minimize trampling, and avoid disturbing wildlife and habitats.

5. **Respect for Private and Protected Lands:**

- Obtain necessary permits and permissions before foraging on private, protected, or restricted lands.

- Show respect for landowners, their property, and adhere to regulations set forth by conservation organizations and governing bodies.

6. **Awareness of Local Laws and Regulations:**

- Familiarize yourself with local laws and regulations related to foraging, especially in protected areas, to ensure compliance and responsible behaviour.

7. **Educational Outreach:**

- Actively engage in educating others about responsible foraging practices, emphasizing the importance of sustainable harvests and ethical behaviour.

- Encourage a community of responsible foragers and share knowledge to collectively make a positive impact.

Sustainability in Foraging:

1. **Understanding Plant Life Cycles:**

- Gain knowledge about the life cycles and growth patterns of the wild edible plants you forage to ensure sustainable practices.

- Harvest in a way that allows the plants to complete their life cycle and reproduce.

2. **Respect for Ecosystems:**

- Consider the broader ecosystem when foraging, ensuring that your actions do not disrupt or harm other species or natural habitats.

- Avoid foraging in sensitive ecosystems or areas with vulnerable flora and fauna.

3. Invasive Species Management:

- Contribute to the control and management of invasive plant species by prioritizing their harvest, which helps native plants, thrive and maintains ecosystem balance.

4. Support for Biodiversity:

- Encourage and support biodiversity by varying the types of wild edible plants you forage and incorporating a wide range of species into your diet.

5. Reforestation and Habitat Restoration:

- Participate in reforestation projects or habitat restoration initiatives as a way to give back and contribute to the environment.

- Volunteer with conservation organizations to help restore natural habitats and ecosystems.

6. **Advocacy for Sustainable Practices:**

- Advocate for sustainable foraging practices within your community and beyond, emphasizing the importance of long-term environmental stewardship

7. **Research and Continuous Learning:**

- Stay informed about the latest research, best practices, and advancements in sustainable foraging to continually improve your approach and minimize environmental impact.

Responsible foraging and sustainability go hand-in-hand, ensuring that wild edible plant harvesting is done in a manner that preserves and enhances the natural world for future generations. By adhering to these principles, foragers can have a positive impact on the environment while enjoying the benefits of wild edibles.

CHAPTER TWO
Essential Foraging Tools and Equipment

Gathering Baskets and Bags

Gathering baskets and bags are indispensable tools for wild edible plant foragers, facilitating the responsible and efficient collection of plants while ensuring minimal environmental impact. These containers are specially designed to safely and conveniently carry harvested wild edibles during foraging expeditions. Let us explore these tools in detail:

1. Purpose and Functionality:

- **Harvest Storage:** Gathering baskets and bags serve as portable containers to store freshly harvested wild edible plants, preventing damage and maintaining their freshness.

- **Organization:** These tools allow foragers to organize different plant varieties, separating them based on type, size, or stage of growth, aiding in identification and later use.

2. Types of Gathering Containers:

- **Baskets:**

    - *Wicker Baskets:* Traditional and eco-friendly, wicker baskets are made from natural materials like willow, bamboo, or rattan, providing ventilation for the plants and allowing them to breathe.

    - *Mesh Baskets:* Baskets with mesh sides or bottoms offer excellent aeration and drainage, preventing moisture build-up and maintaining the quality of the harvest.

    - *Backpack Baskets:* Designed like a backpack, these baskets have compartments and ergonomic features for comfortable and organized carrying.

- **Bags:**

  - *Canvas Bags:* Sturdy and reusable, canvas bags are suitable for carrying a variety of wild edibles, and they can be easily cleaned after use.

  - *Mesh Bags:* Lightweight and breathable, mesh bags allow air circulation, reducing the risk of wilting and preserving the harvested plants' quality.

  - *Nylon or Polyester Bags:* Durable and water-resistant, these bags are ideal for foraging in damp or wet conditions, protecting the contents from moisture.

3. Considerations for Choosing:

- **Durability:** Select containers made from durable materials that can withstand the rigors of outdoor use, ensuring longevity and reliability.

- **Size and Capacity:** Choose a size that matches the intended foraging load, ensuring the container is spacious enough to accommodate the expected quantity of wild edibles without overcrowding.

- **Portability and Comfort:** Opt for containers that are easy to carry, either with handles, straps, or backpack-style designs, distributing weight evenly and providing comfort during foraging trips.

- **Environmentally Friendly:** Prioritize eco-friendly materials that have a minimal environmental impact and can be reused or recycled, aligning with sustainable foraging practices.

4. Maintenance and Cleaning:

- **Regular Cleaning:** After each foraging excursion, clean the basket or bag thoroughly to remove any residual dirt, debris, or plant matter to maintain hygiene and prevent cross-contamination.

- **Drying:** Allow the container to air dry completely to prevent the growth of mold or mildew before storing it for future use.

5. Best Practices:

- **Carry Multiple Containers:** Employ multiple baskets or bags to separate different plant species or to keep plants at varying stages of growth organized, aiding in identification and utilization.

- **Handle with Care:** Handle the gathering container with care to prevent crushing or damaging delicate wild edibles, ensuring they maintain their integrity and flavour.

Gathering baskets and bags are fundamental tools for the ethical and efficient collection of wild edible plants. Choosing the right type and maintaining them properly will enhance the foraging experience and contribute to the sustainability of wild plant populations and ecosystems.

Harvesting Tools

Harvesting tools are essential equipment for wild edible plant foragers, enabling efficient, responsible, and safe gathering of plants from their natural habitats. These tools help ensure a respectful interaction with the environment and the plants being harvested. Let us explore a range of common harvesting tools and their purposes:

1. Hand Tools:

- **Pruning Shears:**

    - *Purpose:* Pruning shears, also known as secateurs, are used to carefully cut stems, branches, or leaves without causing unnecessary harm to the plant.

    - *Application:* Ideal for harvesting larger or tougher plant parts, allowing for a precise and clean cut.

- **Hand Pruners:**

- *Purpose:* Hand pruners are versatile cutting tools used to harvest smaller branches, stems, and leaves.

  - *Application:* Perfect for gathering a variety of wild edibles, they provide a sharp, controlled cut.

- **Grafting Knife:**

  - *Purpose:* A grafting knife with a sharp, thin blade is used for precise cuts during grafting or delicate harvesting tasks.

  - *Application:* Suitable for harvesting tender shoots, buds, or for grafting edible plants to promote growth and variety.

- **Hori Hori or Soil Knife:**

  - *Purpose:* The hori hori is a multi-purpose tool with a serrated blade, ideal for digging, cutting, and harvesting.

- *Application:* Useful for cutting roots, digging up tubers, and slicing through soil to access roots or bulbs.

2. Harvesting Scissors:

- *Purpose:* Harvesting scissors, also known as herb or flower snips are designed for precision cutting and delicate harvesting of small plant parts.

- *Application:* Perfect for harvesting delicate leaves, flowers, herbs, and seeds without damaging the plant.

3. Harvesting Sickles:

- *Purpose:* Sickles have a curved, sharp blade and are used for cutting larger stems and grasses quickly and efficiently.

- *Application:* Suitable for harvesting grains, grasses, and other wild plants with thicker stems.

4. Harvesting Bags and Pouches:

- *Purpose:* Specialized bags and pouches designed for foraging provide a convenient and hands-free way to carry harvested plants.

- *Application:* Allows for easy organization and transportation of different plant varieties while keeping hands free for harvesting.

5. Trowel or Digging Tool:

- *Purpose:* A trowel or digging tool is used for digging up roots, tubers, and bulbs from the ground.

- *Application:* Essential for harvesting plants that grow underground, such as wild onions, roots, or tubers.

6. Gloves:

- *Purpose:* Protective gloves shield hands from thorns, prickles, irritants, or stinging plants during harvesting.

- *Application:* Ensures safety and comfort while handling various plant species, particularly those with protective mechanisms.

7. Bamboo or Wooden Digging Stick:

- *Purpose:* A simple, lightweight tool used for digging or loosening soil during harvesting.

- *Application:* Helpful for accessing plants with shallow roots or gathering plants that grow in compacted soil.

8. Ethical Harvesting Tools:

- *Purpose:* Various ethical tools, such as plant-specific harvesting combs or special traps, are designed to minimize harm and ensure sustainable harvesting practices.

- *Application:* Used for gentle and respectful harvesting, preventing overharvesting and damage to the plant or its surroundings.

9. Multi-Tool or Swiss Army Knife:

- *Purpose:* A compact, versatile tool with multiple functions, including cutting, slicing, and prying.

- *Application:* Useful for a variety of harvesting tasks, providing essential tools in one compact unit.

10. Brush or Whisk Broom:

- *Purpose:* A brush or whiskbroom is used for gently cleaning dirt or debris from harvested plants.

- *Application:* Helps maintain the quality and cleanliness of the harvest before storing or processing.

11. Mushroom Knife:

- *Purpose:* A mushroom knife is designed for safely and efficiently harvesting mushrooms, with a specialized blade and brush.

- *Application:* Used for careful cutting and cleaning of wild mushrooms.

12. Magnifying Glass or Loupe:

- *Purpose:* Magnifying tools aid in plant identification, allowing for a closer examination of key characteristics.

- *Application:* Useful for confirming identification and ensuring accurate harvesting of specific plant species.

Considerations for Choosing Harvesting Tools:

- Consider the plant types you intend to harvest and choose tools accordingly.

- Prioritize durability, ease of use, and ergonomic design to reduce strain during extended foraging sessions.

- Regularly maintain and sharpen cutting tools to ensure efficient and clean cuts, promoting plant health.

Selecting and using the right harvesting tools is crucial for responsible and effective wild edible plant foraging. By employing these tools appropriately, foragers can harvest sustainably, ensuring the preservation of plant populations and the integrity of natural habitats.

Field Guides and Identification Resources

Field guides and identification resources are valuable references used by wild edible plant foragers to accurately identify plants, understand their properties, and distinguish edible species from potentially harmful ones. These resources play a crucial role in safe and responsible foraging. Here's a brief explanation:

1. Field Guides:

- *Description:* Field guides are portable, comprehensive books or digital resources that provide detailed information, illustrations, and photographs of wild plants, including their characteristics, habitat, distribution, and uses.

- *Use:* Foragers carry field guides during expeditions for on-the-spot identification, aiding in determining the edibility and potential uses of the plants encountered.

- *Benefits:* Field guides offer a wealth of knowledge, assisting foragers in confidently identifying plants in diverse environments and ensuring safety and informed decision-making.

2. Mobile Applications:

- *Description:* Mobile applications or apps provide digital field guides accessible through smartphones or tablets, offering a convenient and interactive way to identify plants in the field.

- *Use:* Foragers use these apps to quickly search, identify, and learn about wild plants by entering specific characteristics or utilizing image recognition features.

- *Benefits:* Mobile apps provide real-time assistance, making plant identification more accessible, efficient, and user-friendly for modern foragers.

3. Websites and Online Databases:

- *Description:* Online platforms host vast databases, articles, and resources about wild edible plants, often featuring photographs, descriptions, and user-generated content.

- *Use:* Foragers access these websites to research, cross-reference, and gather information on plant identification, characteristics, distribution, and usage.

- *Benefits:* Online resources offer a wealth of up-to-date information, connect foragers with a community of enthusiasts, and provide a platform for sharing experiences and knowledge.

4. Local Botanical Gardens and Nature Centers:

- *Description:* Local botanical gardens, nature centres, or environmental organizations offer educational programs, workshops, and guided tours focusing on plant identification, including wild edibles.

- *Use:* Foragers participate in these programs to enhance their knowledge, learn from experts, and gain practical experience in plant identification.

- *Benefits:* These organizations provide hands-on learning opportunities, fostering a deeper understanding of local flora and promoting responsible foraging practices.

5. Community Workshops and Events:

- *Description:* Community workshops, gatherings, or events may feature experienced foragers, botanists, or naturalists who share their expertise on plant identification, sustainable foraging, and wild edibles.

- *Use:* Foragers attend these events to learn from experts, network with fellow enthusiasts, and expand their understanding of wild edible plants.

- *Benefits:* Community events encourage learning, collaboration, and the exchange of knowledge among foragers, contributing to a well-informed and responsible foraging community.

Field guides and identification resources are invaluable tools that empower foragers with knowledge, enabling them to confidently identify and utilize wild edible plants while fostering a deeper appreciation for the natural world.

Safety Gear and First Aid Kits

Safety gear and first aid kits are crucial components of a forager's toolkit, prioritizing safety and addressing potential hazards during wild edible plant foraging. These essentials help foragers manage emergencies and unexpected situations effectively. Here is an overview:

1. Safety Gear:

- **Hiking Boots:**
    - *Purpose:* Sturdy hiking boots provide ankle support and protect against sharp objects, ensuring stability and minimizing the risk of injuries while navigating varied terrain.

- **Protective Clothing:**

- *Purpose:* Lightweight, moisture-wicking, and long-sleeved clothing, along with a wide-brimmed hat and sunglasses, shield the skin from sun exposure, insect bites, thorns, and irritants.

- **Gloves:**

  - *Purpose:* Durable gloves safeguard hands from cuts, scratches, thorns, and potential allergens, enhancing grip and reducing contact with harmful plants.

- **Insect Repellent:**

  - *Purpose:* Effective insect repellent helps deter mosquitoes, ticks, and other insects that may transmit diseases or cause discomfort during foraging.

- **Tick Remover Tool:**

  - *Purpose:* A tick remover tool helps safely remove ticks, reducing the risk of tick-borne illnesses prevalent in certain regions.

2. First Aid Kit:

- **Basic First Aid Supplies:**

  - *Components:* Adhesive bandages, antiseptic wipes, gauze, adhesive tape, scissors, tweezers, and a digital thermometer form the foundational elements of a first aid kit.

- **Pain Relief and Anti-inflammatory Medications:**

  - *Components:* Acetaminophen or ibuprofen help manage pain, fever, and minor inflammations.

- **Antihistamines:**

  - *Purpose:* Antihistamines, such as diphenhydramine, counter allergic reactions from insect bites, stings, or plant-induced allergies.

- **EpiPen (Epinephrine Auto-Injector):**

- *Purpose:* Foragers with known severe allergic reactions should carry an EpiPen for immediate treatment of anaphylaxis.

- **Allergy Medications:**

  - *Components:* Antihistamine or decongestant tablets to manage mild allergic reactions or sinus issues caused by pollen or plants.

- **Moleskin or Blister Pads:**

  - *Purpose:* Moleskin and blister pads prevent and manage blisters caused by friction from footwear.

- **Personal Medications:**

  - *Components:* Carry personal medications prescribed by a healthcare professional for dechronic conditions or allergies.

- **Emergency Phone Numbers and Instructions:**

- *Purpose:* Include a list of important emergency contact numbers, allergies, medical conditions, and basic first aid instructions.

Considerations for Safety Gear and First Aid Kits:

- **Customization:** Tailor safety gear and first aid kits to your specific needs, considering your health, allergies, and potential hazards in the foraging area.

- **Regular Check and Restock:** Periodically review and update the contents of the first aid kit to ensure that all items are in good condition and within their expiration dates.

- **Training and Knowledge:** Equip yourself with the knowledge of basic first aid and how to effectively use the items in your first aid kit.

Safety gear and a well-prepared first aid kit are vital for mitigating risks and managing unforeseen situations during wild edible plant foraging, fostering a safe and enjoyable foraging experience.

CHAPTER THREE
Plant Identification and Safety

Identifying Edible vs. Non-Edible Plants: A Concise Guide

Distinguishing between edible and non-edible plants during foraging is paramount for safety and responsible harvesting. Here is a brief but comprehensive guide on how to identify these plants:

1. Positive Identification of Edible Plants:

- **Accurate Identification:**

    - Utilize reliable field guides, online resources, and local e

    - Edible to accurately identify edible plants based on their unique characteristics, such as leaves, stems, flowers, and fruits.

- **Edible Plant Characteristics:**

    - Look for known edible plant features like specific leaf patterns, recognizable flowers,

    - identifiable fruit shapes, and other distinct attributes detailed in reputable guides.

- **Cross-Reference Multiple Sources:**

    - Confirm the plant's identity by cross-referencing information from different reputable sources, including books, apps, websites, and local experts, to minimize the risk of misidentification.

- **Positive Verification:**

    - Verify the plant's edibility with utmost certainty before harvesting or consuming, especially if you are a beginner or unfamiliar with the specific plant.

2. Avoidance of Non-Edible or Toxic Plants:

- **Negative Identification:**

  - Familiarize yourself with common poisonous or toxic plants in your foraging area, learning to recognize their key features and characteristics.

- **Distinctive Non-Edible Plant Traits:**

  - Note features like milky sap, strong or unpleasant odours, thorns, spines, or other clear indicators that often suggest a plant is non-edible or potentially harmful.

- **Caution with Look-Alikes:**

  - Exercise caution with plants that resemble known edible species, especially if you are uncertain, as some non-edible or toxic plants may mimic safe options.

- **Certainty in Identification:**

- If in doubt about a plant's edibility, err on the side of caution and refrain from consuming it. Verify its identity through reliable sources before proceeding.

General Tips:

- **Study Local Flora:**

    - Familiarize yourself with the local flora and prevalent wild edible plants in your region, tailoring your knowledge to the plants you are likely to encounter.

- **Attend Foraging Workshops:**

    - Participate in foraging workshops, guided nature walks, or programs led by experienced foragers or botanists to enhance your plant identification skills.

- **Start with Easy-to-Identify Edibles:**

    - Begin your foraging journey with easily identifiable and widely recognized edible plants, gaining confidence before attempting more advanced identifications.

- **Record and Document:**

  - Maintain a foraging journal, documenting the plants you identify and harvest, along with any experiences or learnings to aid future foraging endeavours.

By honing your skills in identifying edible and non-edible plants through accurate sources and cautious observation, you can forage responsibly and enjoy the bounty of nature safely.

Recognizing Poisonous Plants and Potential Hazards: A Brief Guide

Identifying and recognizing poisonous plants is critical for ensuring the safety and well-being of foragers during wild edible plant expeditions.

Here is a concise yet comprehensive guide to help you recognize potential hazards:

1. Common Features of Poisonous Plants:

- **Unusual Colours or Markings:**
  - Be cautious of plants with unusual, vibrant, or distinct colours, as they can indicate toxicity. Bright red, yellow, or orange hues are often warning signs.

- **Milky or Discoloured Sap:**
  - Plants exuding milky or coloured sap, especially if it's foul-smelling or irritates the skin, are often poisonous.

- **Strong or Unpleasant Odours:**
  - Plants emitting strong or disagreeable odours, particularly akin to almonds, garlic, or rotten smells, can be toxic.

- **Spines, Thorns, or Hairs:**
  - Plants covered in spines, thorns, or irritating hairs may be harmful and

should be handled with care or avoided.

- **Bitter Taste:**

    - A bitter or acrid taste in a plant is a common warning sign of potential toxicity.

2. Cautionary Measures:

- **Avoidance of Unknown Plants:**

    - Refrain from consuming any wild plant if you are unsure of its edibility or safety.

- **Handling Precautions:**

    - Exercise caution when handling unfamiliar plants; avoid touching your face or eyes after handling them.

- **Keep Children Informed:**

    - Educate children about the potential dangers of consuming unknown plants, emphasizing not to touch or taste any plant without adult supervision.

- **Beware of Look-Alikes:**

    - Be cautious of plants that closely resemble known edible species but may be poisonous. Always verify their identity before consumption.

3. Educational Resources:

- **Field Guides and Apps:**

    - Utilize reliable field guides, mobile apps, or reputable online resources dedicated to identifying and providing information about poisonous plants in your region.

- **Local Botanists or Experts:**

    - Seek guidance from local experts, botanists, or agricultural extension services to identify and learn about poisonous plants in your specific area.

- **Community Workshops:**

- Attend workshops or seminars focused on identifying toxic plants and potential hazards associated with wild foraging.

4. Specific Poisonous Plants to Watch For:

- **Poison Ivy, Oak, and Sumac:**

  - Learn to recognize these common poisonous plants, characterized by their distinctive leaves and ability to cause skin irritation upon contact.

- **Deadly Nightshade (Belladonna):**

  - Recognize the dark, shiny berries and bell-shaped flowers of deadly nightshade, a highly toxic plant.

- **Castor Bean Plant:**

  - Identify the large, spiky seedpods and distinctive leaves of the castor bean plant, which contains ricin, a potent toxin.

- **Foxglove:**

- Be cautious of the tubular, brightly coloured flowers of foxglove, which contain cardiac glycosides and can be lethal if ingested.

By familiarizing yourself with these indicators and potential poisonous plants, you can navigate wild areas safely and make informed decisions to avoid potential hazards. Always prioritize caution and verification when dealing with unfamiliar flora.

Common Wild Edible Plants: Identification and Characteristics

Identifying and understanding common wild edible plants is a fundamental aspect of foraging for sustenance and connecting with nature. Here is a brief professional overview of identifying and understanding the characteristics of some prevalent wild edible plants:

1. Dandelion (*Taraxacum officinale*):

- **Identification:** Recognizable by its yellow flowers and distinct toothed leaves in a basal rosette.

- **Characteristics:** Entire plant is edible - leaves are bitter and nutrient-rich, flowers can be used for tea or salads, roots can be roasted for a coffee substitute.

2. Stinging Nettle (*Urtica dioica*):

- **Identification:** Has serrated leaves with stinging hairs that cause skin irritation upon contact.

- **Characteristics:** Young leaves are edible when cooked or dried; rich in vitamins, minerals, and can be used in soups, teas, or steamed.

3. Wild Garlic (*Allium ursinum*):

- **Identification:** Features clusters of star-like white flowers and a strong garlic smell when crushed.

- **Characteristics:** Leaves and bulbs are edible, offering a mild garlic flavour; used in salads, pesto, or cooked dishes.

4. Plantain (*Plantago major*):

- **Identification:** Broad, ribbed leaves in a basal rosette, often found in disturbed areas.

- **Characteristics:** Leaves are edible and rich in vitamins and minerals; can be consumed raw in salads or cooked in soups.

5. Chickweed (*Stellaria media*):

- **Identification:** Small, delicate leaves with tiny white flowers, often forming dense mats.

- **Characteristics:** Tender leaves are edible raw or cooked, offering a mild flavour; can be used in salads, sandwiches, or cooked dishes.

6. Berries (Various Types):

- **Identification:** Varied depending on the type; common wild berries include blackberries, blueberries, raspberries, and strawberries.

- **Characteristics:** Edible and highly nutritious, rich in vitamins, antioxidants, and fibre; often consumed fresh, in jams, or used for baking.

Key Considerations for Identification:

- Utilize reliable field guides, online resources, or seek guidance from experienced foragers to accurately identify wild edible plants.

- Pay attention to leaf shape, colour, arrangement, flowers, fruits, and habitat to distinguish between different species.

- Exercise caution and positively identify plants before consumption, ensuring they are indeed edible and not poisonous look-alikes.

By familiarizing oneself with these common wild edible plants and their distinctive features, foragers can confidently identify, harvest, and incorporate them into their diets, enhancing both nutrition and connection with the natural environment.

CHAPTER FOUR

Foraging Ethics and Best Practices

Sustainable Foraging Guidelines: Balancing Harvesting and Conservation

Sustainable foraging refers to the practice of gathering wild plants, fungi, and other natural resources in a manner that ensures the long-term health and vitality of the ecosystem. This approach emphasizes responsible harvesting, conservation, and minimizing negative impacts on the environment. Here are the key guidelines for sustainable foraging:

1. Know the Regulations:

- Familiarize yourself with local laws, regulations, and guidelines related to foraging in specific areas. Adhere to designated rules to prevent overharvesting and maintain the delicate balance of the ecosystem.

2. Respect Seasons and Life Cycles:

- Harvest wild edibles during their respective seasons and growth stages. Avoid harvesting during critical periods such as flowering or seed dispersal to allow plants to reproduce and replenish.

3. Selective Harvesting:

- Practice selective harvesting by taking only a small portion of a plant population, ensuring its ability to regenerate and sustain itself. Focus on abundant species and leave rare or threatened plants untouched.

4. Ethical Harvesting:

- Respect private property and obtain necessary permits for foraging. Seek landowner permissions and adhere to ethical foraging principles when on public or private lands.

5. Avoid Overharvesting:

- Avoid depleting a specific area of its wild edibles by limiting the quantity you harvest. Allow plants to thrive and continue growing for future generations.

6. Leave No Trace:

- Adhere to the "Leave No Trace" principles by cleaning up after yourself, disposing of waste properly, and avoiding any damage to the natural habitat. Minimize your impact on the environment.

7. Forage Invasive Species:

- Focus on harvesting invasive plant species to help control their populations and protect native flora. This contributes to ecosystem balance and promotes biodiversity.

8. Responsible Foraging Tools:

- Use appropriate, non-invasive tools for harvesting and gathering, minimizing harm

to plants and their habitats. Opt for tools
designed for sustainable foraging practices.

9. Educate and Share Knowledge:

- Educate yourself and others about
  sustainable foraging practices, encouraging
  responsible behaviour and the preservation
  of wild edibles. Share knowledge within
  communities to create a culture of
  responsible foragers.

10. Contribute to Conservation:

- Support conservation efforts by
  volunteering for habitat restoration
  projects, reforestation initiatives, or
  invasive species removal programs. Give
  back to the environment and contribute to
  its sustainability.

11. Document and Record:

- Keep records of your foraging activities,
  documenting what, when, and where you
  harvested. This helps in tracking your

impact and improving sustainability in the end.

Sustainable foraging embraces a holistic approach that respects both nature and local communities. By following these guidelines, foragers can enjoy the benefits of wild edibles while ensuring the preservation and future abundance of these valuable natural resources.

Leave No Trace Principles: Minimizing Environmental Impact

"Leave No Trace" (LNT) is a set of outdoor ethics that provides guidelines on how to minimize human affect and preserve the wilderness for future generations. These principles aim to ensure responsible recreation and a deeper connection with nature. Here is a brief overview:

1. Plan and Prepare:

- *Anticipate Needs:* Thoroughly plan trips, considering factors like weather, terrain, group size, and skill levels to reduce the likelihood of accidents and emergencies.

2. Travel and Camp on Durable Surfaces:

- *Stay on Designated Trails:* Stick to established paths to avoid trampling on vegetation and causing soil erosion.

- *Camp Responsibly:* Set up campsites on durable surfaces like established sites, rock, or gravel to minimize damage to the ecosystem.

3. Dispose of Waste Properly:

- Pack Out: Carry out all trash, leftover food, and litter. Leave with everything you brought into the wilderness.

- Properly Dispose of Human Waste: Use designated facilities or dig small holes at least 200 feet from water sources to bury human waste.

4. Leave What You Find:

- *Preserve Nature:* Avoid picking plants, disturbing historical or cultural sites, or altering natural features. Leave rocks, plants, and other natural item or objects as you found them.

5. Minimize Campfire Impact:

- *Use Stoves Instead:* Whenever possible, use a portable stove for cooking instead of building a fire. If you must have a fire, use established fire rings and keep it small.

6. Respect Wildlife:

- *Observe from a Distance:* Do not approach or feed wildlife; respect their space and observe them from a safe distance.

- *Store Food Safely:* Store food and scented items securely to avoid attracting wildlife to your campsite.

7. Be Considerate of Other Visitors:

- *Yield to Others:* Hikers going uphill have the right of way. Be courteous and yield to others on the trail.

- *Keep Noise Levels down:* Avoid loud noises and respect the serenity of the wilderness.

8. Educate Yourself and Others:

- *Learn and Share:* Educate yourself about the area you plan to visit and share Leave No Trace principles with fellow outdoor enthusiasts to promote responsible recreation.

By following these Leave No Trace principles, outdoor enthusiasts can enjoy nature while minimizing their impact, fostering a sense of responsibility and sustainability, and preserving the beauty of the outdoors for future generations.

Respecting Wildlife and Ecosystems: A Harmony between Nature and Humanity

Respecting wildlife and ecosystems is a fundamental principle in fostering a balanced and sustainable coexistence between humans and the natural world. It involves understanding, appreciating, and protecting the diverse life forms and habitats that make up our planet. Here is a brief exploration of how we can achieve this harmony:

1. Educate Yourself and Others:

- *Learn About Local Wildlife:* Understand the behaviour, habitats, and needs of wildlife in the area you visit. Knowledge promotes informed and respectful interactions.

2. Observe from a Distance:

- *Practice Responsible Wildlife Viewing:* Admire wildlife from a safe and respectful distance, using binoculars or zoom lenses to avoid causing stress or disturbance.

3. Avoid Feeding Wildlife:

- *Resist the Temptation:* Do not feed wild animals, as it disrupts their natural diets, behaviour, and can lead to dependency on humans.

4. Dispose of Waste Properly:

- *Mindful Trash Disposal:* Properly dispose of trash and litter to prevent wildlife from ingesting harmful substances. Carry out what you carry in.

5. Stay on Designated Trails:

- *Prevent Habitat Damage:* Stick to designated paths to minimize trampling on vegetation and disturbing habitats.

6. Leave What You Find:

- *Preserve Natural Features:* Avoid picking plants, removing rocks, or disrupting the environment. Leave everything as you found it.

7. Reduce Noise Levels:

- *Maintain Tranquility:* Keep noise levels down to prevent disturbing wildlife and other visitors. The natural soundscape is an essential part of the ecosystem.

8. Respect Wildlife's Nocturnal Habits:

- *Minimize Night-time Disturbance:* If exploring at night, use minimal artificial lighting to respect the nocturnal activities of wildlife.

9. Support Conservation Efforts:

- *Donate and Volunteer:* Contribute to organizations and initiatives focused on conserving wildlife and habitats.

10. Promote Responsible Tourism:

- *Choose Responsible Tour Operators:* Opt for tour operators who prioritize sustainable practices and wildlife conservation in their activities.

11. Be a Responsible Pet Owner:

- *Control Pets:* If allowed, keep pets on a leash to prevent them from disturbing wildlife and habitats.

12. Report Violations:

- *Be a Watchful Guardian:* Report any wildlife harassment, poaching, or habitat destruction to the appropriate authorities.

Respecting wildlife and ecosystems is about recognizing our interconnectedness with all living beings and ecosystems. By embracing responsible and mindful actions, we ensure that future generations can cherish and enjoy the natural world in its full splendour.

Legal Considerations and Permits for Wild Edible Plant Foraging

Foraging for wild edible plants is an enjoyable and sustainable activity, but it is important to adhere to legal regulations and obtain any required permits to ensure that you are foraging responsibly and legally. Here is a brief overview of the legal aspects and permits related to wild edible plant foraging:

1. Know the Laws and Regulations:

- **Local Laws:** Research and understand the laws and regulations governing foraging in your region. Regulations can vary by country, state, or even local municipalities.

- **Protected Areas:** Be aware of protected areas, national parks, reserves, or private lands where foraging may be restricted or prohibited.

2. Permits for Foraging:

- **Check Requirements:** Some regions may require permits for foraging, especially in protected areas. Check with the local authorities or landowners to determine if a permit is needed.

- **Permit Application Process:** If permits are required, understand the application process, associated fees, and any specific conditions or restrictions.

3. Private Property and Landowner Permissions:

- **Obtain Permission:** If you plan to forage on private property, obtain explicit permission from the landowner to ensure legal access and avoid trespassing.

4. Seasonal and Quantity Restrictions:

- **Respect Seasons:** Abide by seasonal restrictions on harvesting certain plants to allow for natural propagation and growth.

- **Quantity Limits:** Some areas may have restrictions on the quantity of plants you can harvest to prevent overexploitation.

5. Ethical Foraging Practices:

- **Follow Ethical Guidelines:** Adhere to ethical foraging practices, such as leaving no trace, respecting wildlife, and minimizing your impact on the environment.

6. Protected or Endangered Species:

- **Be Informed:** Familiarize yourself with lists of protected or endangered plant species, and avoid harvesting them to support conservation efforts.

7. Local Community Regulations:

- **Check Community Rules:** Some communities may have specific regulations regarding foraging in certain areas or for particular plant species. Always respect local guidelines.

8. Participate in Guided Tours or Workshops:

- **Consider Guided Tours:** Joining guided foraging tours led by certified professionals can ensure you operate within legal boundaries and learn about responsible foraging.

9. Stay Informed and Updated:

- **Regularly Check Regulations:** Stay informed about any changes in laws or regulations related to foraging in your area and adjust your practices accordingly.

Adhering to legal considerations and obtaining any necessary permits ensures that your foraging activities are in compliance with local laws and regulations, contributing to the responsible and sustainable practice of enjoying the benefits of wild edible plants

CHAPTER FIVE
Harvesting and Preparation

Timing the Harvest

Timing the harvest of wild edible plants is a critical factor that greatly influences the quality, flavour, nutritional value, and sustainability of your foraging efforts. Here is a brief guide on understanding the importance of timing and how to determine the optimal time for harvesting:

1. Plant Growth Stages:

- **Seedling Stage:** Some plants are best harvested in their seedling stage when they are tender and have a mild flavour.

- **Vegetative Stage:** Many leafy greens and herbs are ideal for harvest during this stage, just before flowering, as they are at their most flavourful and nutritious.

2. Flowering and Fruiting:

- **Flowering Stage:** Some edible flowers are best harvested just as they bloom, when their flavours are most pronounced and aromatic.

- **Fruiting Stage:** Harvest fruits when they are fully ripe, ensuring optimal sweetness, texture, and seed development.

3. Seasonal Considerations:

- **Spring:** Spring is often abundant with tender, young shoots, leaves, and flowers of various plants.

- **Summer:** Many plants are at their peak in summer, offering a wide range of fruits, vegetables, and greens.

- **Fall:** Root vegetables and certain fruits reach their prime during the fall, making it an excellent time for harvest.

4. Time of Day:

- **Morning or Evening:** Harvest during the cooler parts of the day, like early morning or evening, to retain the plant's moisture and flavour.

5. Weather Conditions:

- **Dry Days:** Harvest after a few dry days to minimize the risk of mold or bacterial growth on the plants.

- **Avoid Rainy Days:** Avoid harvesting on rainy days to prevent excess moisture and potential contamination.

6. Life Cycle of the Plant:

- **Annuals:** Harvest annual plants before they complete their life cycle to ensure they are at their peak for consumption.

- **Perennials:** Perennial plants can often be harvested over an extended period, allowing for multiple harvests in a season.

7. Responsible Harvesting:

- **Sustainable Practices:** Harvest in a way that ensures the survival and regeneration of the plant population, allowing for future bountiful harvests.

8. Local Knowledge and Experience:

- **Learn from Locals:** Tap into the knowledge of local foragers, farmers, or indigenous communities who have a deep understanding of the optimal harvest times in your region.

Timing the harvest correctly ensures that you obtain the best flavour and nutritional value from wild edible plants while contributing to the sustainability and health of the ecosystem. Always approach harvesting with care, respecting the plants and the environment they thrive in.

Proper Harvesting Techniques

Harvesting wild edible plants with care and precision is vital to maximize yield, preserve the environment, and maintain the plants' regenerative capabilities. Here is a succinct guide on employing proper harvesting techniques:

1. Use Clean and Sharp Tools:

- **Clean Equipment:** Ensure your harvesting tools, such as knives or scissors are clean and free of any residues or contaminants.

- **Sharp Blades:** Use sharp blades to make clean cuts, minimizing damage to the plants and promoting faster healing.

2. Selective Harvesting:

- **Focus on Abundance:** Harvest plants that are abundant in the area, leaving behind the majority to allow for natural replenishment.

- **Avoid Overharvesting:** Be mindful not to deplete an area of its plants. Leave enough to support the population's sustainability.

3. Harvest Responsibly:

- **Leave No Trace:** Tread lightly and avoid damaging surrounding plants, soil, or habitats during the harvest.

- **Respect Growth Points:** Avoid harvesting the central growing point of a plant, as this is essential for future growth.

4. Timing and Growth Stages:

- **Harvest at Optimal Times:** Choose the appropriate growth stage for each plant, ensuring the best flavour, texture, and nutritional value.

- **Avoid Stressing the Plant:** Avoid harvesting during extreme weather conditions or when the plant is stressed, as this can affect its health.

5. Handle with Care:

- **Minimize Bruising:** Handle harvested plants gently to prevent bruising, which can affect their quality and shelf life.

- **Protect Delicate Parts:** Be especially careful with fragile parts like flowers and leaves to maintain their integrity.

6. Clean and Sort Harvested Plants:

- **Clean Thoroughly:** Rinse harvested plants in clean water to remove any dirt, insects, or debris before consumption or storage.

- **Sort for Quality:** Discard any damaged, diseased, or spoiled parts to ensure the harvested plants are of the highest quality.

7. Storage and Preservation:

- **Proper Storage:** Store harvested plants in airtight containers, refrigerate if needed, or use drying techniques to extend shelf life and maintain freshness.

- **Label and Date:** Clearly label the storage containers with the plant name and harvest date for easy identification and organization.

8. Respect Local Regulations:

- **Adhere to Local Laws:** Always follow local laws and regulations regarding foraging, harvesting, and any restrictions on specific plants.

9. Continuous Learning:

- **Expand Knowledge:** Continuously educate yourself on different wild plants, their growth patterns, and optimal harvesting techniques to enhance your foraging skills.

By applying proper harvesting techniques, foragers can sustainably enjoy the benefits of wild edible plants, ensuring a bountiful harvest while preserving the delicate balance of the ecosystem. Responsible and informed harvesting practices contribute to a more sustainable and enriching foraging experience.

Cleaning, Processing, and Storing Wild Edibles: A Comprehensive Guide

After a fruitful foraging expedition, it is essential to handle the wild edibles properly through thorough cleaning, efficient processing, and appropriate storage. These steps ensure the preservation of their flavours, nutritional value, and safety. Here is a detailed guide on how to clean, process, and store wild edibles:

1. Cleaning:

- **Rinse under Cold Water:**

- Gently rinse the harvested wild edibles under cold running water to remove dirt, insects, and debris.

- **Soak in Salt Water:**

  - For certain wild plants, soak them in a bowl of cold water with a pinch of salt to dislodge any hidden insects or impurities.

- **Inspect Thoroughly:**

  - Inspect each piece for signs of damage, spoilage, or unwanted insects. Discard any spoiled or questionable parts.

- **Pat Dry:**

  - After rinsing, gently pat them dry with a clean kitchen towel or paper towel to remove excess moisture.

2. Processing:

- **Trimming and Sorting:**

- Trim off damaged or bruised parts and sort the wild edibles based on their type and intended use.

- **Drying:**

    - Air Dry: Spread the cleaned wild edibles on clean towels or drying racks in a well-ventilated area away from direct sunlight. Turn them occasionally for even drying.

    - Dehydrator: Use a food dehydrator according to the specific requirements of the plant to efficiently dry them while preserving flavours and nutrients.

- **Blanching (for some vegetables):**

    - Briefly blanch certain wild vegetables by immersing them in boiling water for a short time, followed by an ice bath. This helps maintain colour, texture, and nutritional value before freezing.

- **Fermentation (for some plants):**

  - Ferment wild edibles like certain leaves or vegetables in a brine solution to enhance flavour and preserve them. Follow a suitable fermentation process.

3. Storing:

- **Airtight Containers:**

  - Store fully dried wild edibles in airtight containers such as glass jars, airtight bags, or vacuum-sealed packages to prevent moisture and maintain freshness.

- **Labelling:**

  - Label each container with the plant name and date of processing for easy identification.

- **Refrigeration:**

  - Store processed wild edibles in the refrigerator if they are not fully dried, using airtight containers to prolong freshness and prevent spoilage.

- **Freezing:**

  - Freeze processed wild edibles in portions using airtight freezer bags or containers to maintain quality and flavour.

4. Using Processed Wild Edibles:

- **Rehydration:**

  - Rehydrate dried plants by soaking them in water or adding them directly to soups, stews, or other dishes.

- **Incorporate into Recipes:**

  - Use wild edibles in various recipes, including salads, stir-fries, soups, sauces, or as garnishes to enhance flavours and nutrition.

- **Create Extracts or Tinctures:**

  - Utilize wild plants to create extracts, tinctures, or oils for medicinal or culinary purposes, preserving their essential properties.

By following these comprehensive steps for cleaning, processing, and storing wild edibles, foragers can enjoy the extended freshness and utilization of their harvest while exploring a variety of culinary and medicinal applications throughout the year.

Preparing and Cooking Wild Edible Plants

Preparing and cooking wild edible plants is an art that combines culinary creativity with a deep respect for nature's offerings. Proper preparation and cooking techniques ensure that the flavours and nutritional benefits of these wild plants are maximized while maintaining their integrity. Here is a comprehensive guide on how to prepare and cook wild edible plants:

1. Sorting and Cleaning:

- **Thorough Cleaning:** Begin by cleaning wild edibles as previously described to remove any impurities, insects, or debris.

2. Trimming and Cutting:

- **Remove Undesirable Parts:** Trim and discard any damaged, wilted, or unwanted parts of the plants.

- **Cut to Desired Size:** Cut the cleaned plants into the desired size and shape based on the recipe and your preference.

3. Basic Cooking Techniques:

- **Sautéing:**

  - Heat a pan with a small amount of oil or butter. Add the prepared wild edibles and cook briefly until tender. Season to taste.

- **Boiling:**

  - Boil wild edibles in a pot of water until they reach the desired tenderness.

Drain and use in various dishes or season accordingly.

- **Steaming:**

  - Steam the wild edibles in a steamer basket over boiling water until they are tender and cooked to your liking.

- **Grilling or Roasting:**

  - Toss the wild edibles with olive oil, salt, and pepper, then grill or roast them until they are slightly charred and tender.

- **Blanching:**

  - Briefly blanch the wild edibles in boiling water, followed by an ice bath to preserve colour, texture, and nutritional value.

4. Incorporating into Dishes:

- **Salads:**

  - Add fresh or cooked wild edibles to salads, combining them with other

vegetables, nuts, seeds, and a
flavourful dressing.

- **Stir-Fries:**

  - Incorporate wild edibles into stir-fries
    with a variety of vegetables, proteins,
    and seasonings.

- **Soups and Stews:**

  - Include wild edibles in soups, stews, or
    broths for added flavour and nutrition.

- **Sautéed Side Dishes:**

  - Sauté wild edibles with garlic, onions,
    or other aromatics for a flavourful side
    dish.

- **Pasta or Rice Dishes:**

  - Mix wild edibles into pasta or rice
    dishes to enhance the taste and
    nutritional profile.

5. Flavour Enhancements:

- **Seasoning:**

- Use a variety of herbs, spices, and seasonings to enhance the natural flavours of wild edibles.

- **Lemon or Vinegar:**

  - Brighten up the flavours with a squeeze of lemon juice or a splash of vinegar.

- **Nuts and Seeds:**

  - Incorporate toasted nuts or seeds for added crunch and richness.

6. Creative Recipes:

- **Wild Edible Pesto:**

  - Blend wild edibles with garlic, nuts, cheese, olive oil, and seasoning to make a flavourful pesto for pasta or as a spread.

- **Wild Edible Fritters:**

  - Mix wild edibles with a batter of flour, eggs, and seasoning, then fry to make delicious fritters.

- **Infused Oils or Vinegars:**

    - Infuse oils or vinegars with wild edibles to create flavoured bases for dressings and marinades.

7. Experiment and Enjoy:

- **Be Adventurous:**

    - Experiment with different wild edibles, cooking methods, and recipes to discover new flavours and culinary possibilities.

- **Pairing and Combinations:**

    - Pair wild edibles with complementary ingredients to create balanced and delectable dishes.

By following these preparation and cooking guidelines, foragers can unlock the full potential of wild edible plants, savouring their unique flavours and reaping the nutritional benefits while exploring the diverse culinary world of wild foraged cuisine.

CHAPTER SIX
Safety Measures and Emergency Protocols

Handling Emergencies in the Field

Being prepared to handle emergencies while in the field, especially in outdoor or remote settings, is paramount for ensuring the safety and well-being of yourself and others. Whether you are on a hiking trip, camping, or engaged in any outdoor activity, having the knowledge and equipment to manage emergencies is crucial. Here is a detailed guide on handling emergencies in the field:

1. Preparation and Prevention:

- **Trip Planning:**

- Thoroughly research the area you plan to visit, including potential hazards, weather forecasts, and terrain.

  - Share your itinerary with someone you trust, detailing your plans and expected return.

- **Training and Knowledge:**

  - Acquire basic first aid and CPR training from reputable organizations.

  - Learn about the specific risks and potential emergencies associated with the environment you will be in.

- **Emergency Contact Information:**

  - Have a list of emergency contacts saved in your phone and a printed copy in your first aid kit.

- **First Aid Kit:**

  - Carry a well-equipped first aid kit containing essential supplies for treating injuries and medical conditions.

- **Navigation and Communication:**

  - Carry a map, compass, or GPS device to help you navigate and know your location in case of an emergency.

  - Ensure your mobile phone is charged and have a backup power source or portable charger.

2. Common Outdoor Emergencies and Responses:

- **Injuries:**

  - **Response:** Administer first aid for the specific injury; if severe, seek professional medical help.

- **Dehydration and Heat Exhaustion:**

  - **Response:** Rest in shade, hydrate, and cool down. Replenish electrolytes with oral rehydration solutions.

- **Hypothermia:**

- **Response:** Shelter from the cold, change into dry clothes, warm up with blankets or a fire, and consume warm fluids.

- **Wild Animal Encounters:**

  - **Response:** Maintain a safe distance, make noise, and follow guidelines for the specific type of encounter (e.g., bear encounter).

- **Lost or Disoriented:**

  - **Response:** Stay calm, use navigation tools to reorient yourself, and backtrack to a known location if possible.

3. Emergency Protocols:

- **Assess the Situation:**

  - Quickly assess the severity of the emergency and prioritize actions based on the situation.

- **Communicate:**

- Alert emergency services or designated contacts about the situation and location.

- **Administer First Aid:**

  - Utilize your first aid skills and supplies to stabilize and provide immediate care to the injured.

- **Evacuation or Shelter:**

  - Determine if evacuation or seeking shelter is necessary based on the severity of the emergency.

- **Follow Emergency Plan:**

  - Refer to your emergency action plan for specific steps and guidance.

4. Stay Calm and Reassure:

- **Stay Calm:**

  - Maintaining a calm demeanour helps in making rational decisions and aiding others effectively.

- **Reassure Others:**

- Provide reassurance and clear instructions to anyone involved, keeping them informed and calm.

5. Seek Professional Help:

- If the situation is beyond your ability to manage, promptly seek professional medical help or emergency services.

6. Continuous Learning:

- Regularly update your knowledge of first aid techniques and emergency procedures through training and practice.

Being prepared and knowing how to handle emergencies in the field can significantly reduce risks and ensure a safer and more enjoyable outdoor experience. Always prioritize safety, prepare adequately, and be ready to respond effectively to any unexpected situations.

Seeking Professional Medical Help

In any emergency, seeking professional medical help is a crucial step to ensure the best possible outcome for the affected individuals. Professional medical assistance provides expertise, resources, and appropriate treatment necessary to address injuries, illnesses, or severe conditions. Here is a detailed guide on how to seek professional medical help during emergencies:

1. Assess the Situation:

- **Evaluate the Severity:**

    - Determine the severity of the injury or condition to decide if professional medical help is needed.

- **Consider Immediate Risks:**

    - Assess if the situation poses immediate life-threatening risks that require immediate attention.

2. Contact Emergency Services:

- **Call the Local Emergency Number:**

    - In many countries, the emergency number is 911 or a similar designated number. Use it to reach emergency services.

- **Provide Essential Information:**

    - Clearly communicate the nature of the emergency, the location, the number of individuals involved, and any specific details needed for an effective response.

3. Follow Dispatcher Instructions:

- **Listen Carefully:**

    - Follow the dispatcher's instructions carefully and provide any additional information requested.

- **Stay on the Line:**

    - Stay on the call until the dispatcher advises you to hang up. They may provide further guidance or reassess the situation.

4. Arrange for Transport to a Medical Facility:

- **Ambulance Services:**

  - If necessary, request an ambulance to transport the injured or affected individuals to the nearest hospital or medical facility.

- **Provide Clear Directions:**

  - If the location is remote or challenging to find, provide clear directions to assist the ambulance team.

5. Reach the Nearest Medical Facility:

- **Transport by Vehicle:**

  - If possible, safely transport the injured individual to the nearest hospital or medical facility if the situation allows.

- **Communication with Medical Staff:**

- Inform the medical staff of the situation and any relevant information to expedite the necessary care.

6. Cooperate with Medical Professionals:

- **Provide Information:**

  - Offer details about the incident, medical history, allergies, medications, or any other relevant information to aid in appropriate treatment.

- **Follow Medical Advice:**

  - Comply with the medical professionals' recommendations and instructions regarding treatment and further care.

7. Advocate for the Affected Individual:

- **Stay Involved:**

  - Stay informed about the medical condition and treatment plan, advocating for the affected individual to ensure they receive appropriate care.

- **Ask Questions:**

  - Do not hesitate to ask questions or seek clarification to understand the medical situation and the recommended course of action.

8. Keep Records:

- **Document Details:**

  - Maintain a record of the incident, medical treatment, names of medical staff, and any prescribed medications.

- **Share with Follow-Up Care Providers:**

  - Share these records with subsequent medical care providers for continuity of care.

In any emergency, prioritizing seeking professional medical help can be a life-saving decision. Quick and efficient communication with emergency services and subsequent collaboration with medical professionals significantly improve the chances of a positive outcome for those affected. Always be prepared to take this crucial step in emergencies.

CHAPTER SEVEN
Advanced Foraging Techniques

Advanced Plant Identification Skills

Mastering advanced plant identification skills is fundamental for botanists, ecologists, horticulturists, foragers, and nature enthusiasts. It involves a deep understanding of plant anatomy, taxonomy, and ecological contexts. Here is a detailed guide to advance your plant identification skills:

1. Botanical Taxonomy:

- **Study Taxonomic Hierarchies:**

  - Understand the levels of classification (e.g., kingdom, phylum, class, order, family, genus, and species) and how they relate to each other.

- **Learn Plant Families:**

- Study major plant families and their
  characteristics, as many plants within
  a family share common traits.

- **Morphological Characteristics:**

  - Master the identification of plants
    based on their morphological
    features, such as leaves, flowers,
    stems, fruits, and roots.

2. Plant Anatomy:

- **Microscopic Examination:**

  - Develop skills in using microscopes to
    examine plant tissues at a cellular
    level, aiding in identification.

- **Tissue Types:**

  - Understand different types of plant
    tissues (e.g., epidermal, ground,
    vascular) and their roles.

- **Leaf Morphology:**

- Study leaf anatomy, including types of venation, margins, arrangements, and adaptations.

3. Plant Adaptations:

- **Ecological Adaptations:**

  - Learn how plants adapt to different environmental conditions, such as xerophytes (drought-tolerant plants) and hydrophytes (aquatic plants).

- **Specialized Structures:**

  - Understand specialized structures like succulents, aerenchyma, and thorns that help plants adapt to specific environments.

4. Ecological Context:

- **Habitat Identification:**

  - Master identifying plants based on the habitats they thrive in, including forests, grasslands, wetlands, etc.

- **Ecosystem Interactions:**

- Understand plant interactions with other organisms, like pollinators, herbivores, and symbiotic relationships.

5. Use of Identification Keys:

- **Flora and Field Guides:**

    - Utilize advanced plant identification keys found in botanical field guides or floras specific to your region.

- **Digital Identification Tools:**

    - Use online platforms and apps that offer advanced plant identification using photos and descriptions.

6. Field Botany and Herbarium Skills:

- **Field Collection:**

    - Learn proper techniques for collecting plant specimens, including pressing, drying, and labelling.

- **Herbarium Visits:**

- Visit herbaria to understand how plant collections are organized and study preserved specimens.

- **Specimen Identification:**

  - Practice identifying dried plant specimens using field guides and comparing them with known specimens.

7. Plant Dichotomous Keys:

- **Understand Key Structure:**

  - Learn how to use dichotomous keys, which present a series of choices leading to the correct identification of a plant.

- **Practice with Real Keys:**

  - Work through published dichotomous keys to improve your ability to use them effectively.

8. Continual Learning:

- **Stay Updated:**

- Keep up with the latest botanical research, taxonomic changes, and advancements in plant identification methodologies.

- **Participate in Workshops:**

  - Attend workshops, seminars, and botanical courses to learn from experts and gain hands-on experience.

9. Join Botanical Communities:

- **Local Botanical Societies:**

  - Join local botanical societies or online forums to connect with fellow enthusiasts and professionals, sharing knowledge and experiences.

- **Volunteer Opportunities:**

  - Participate in volunteer projects or citizen science initiatives related to plant identification and conservation.

10. Field Experience:

- **Guided Field Trips:**

- Join guided plant identification field trips led by experts to enhance your skills and gain practical knowledge.

- **Practice Observation:**

  - Develop keen observational skills by spending time in nature, closely observing and documenting plant characteristics.

11. Ethnobotany:

- **Study Plant Uses:**

  - Explore the traditional uses of plants by different cultures, including medicinal, culinary, and cultural applications.

- **Understanding Plant Relationships:**

  - Learn how plants have been historically used and valued by communities, connecting it to their identification and taxonomy.

Mastering advanced plant identification skills involves a combination of theoretical knowledge, practical experience, and a passion for understanding the botanical world. Continuous learning, hands-on practice, and engagement with the broader botanical community will deepen your understanding and proficiency in plant identification.

Wild Edible Plant Preservation and Fermentation

Preservation and fermentation of wild edible plants allow you to extend their shelf life, enhance their flavours, and retain their nutritional value. These techniques have been practiced for generations, and they offer a way to enjoy wild edibles throughout the year. Here is a detailed guide on preserving and fermenting wild edible plants:

1. Drying:

- **Harvest at the Right Time:**

- Harvest the wild edible plants at their peak freshness, ensuring the best flavour and nutrient content.

- **Clean and Prepare:**

  - Clean the plants thoroughly, removing dirt and debris. Trim any unwanted parts.

- **Air Drying:**

  - Spread the cleaned plants in a single layer on trays or hang them in a well-ventilated area away from direct sunlight to dry.

- **Dehydrator:**

  - Use a food dehydrator set to the appropriate temperature to dry the plants quickly and evenly.

- **Store Properly:**

  - Once dried, store the plants in airtight containers away from moisture and light to maintain their quality.

2. Freezing:

- **Blanching:**
    - Blanch the wild edible plants by briefly immersing them in boiling water, followed by an ice bath to stop the cooking process.
- **Drain and Pack:**
    - Drain excess water and pack the blanched plants into airtight freezer-safe containers or vacuum-sealed bags.
- **Freeze:**
    - Place the packed plants in the freezer, ensuring they are not overcrowded, to maintain their quality and freshness.

3. Canning:

- **Prepare Jars:**
    - Sterilize glass canning jars and lids by boiling them or using a dishwasher.
- **Process the Plants:**

- Pack the cleaned and prepared wild edibles into the sterilized jars, leaving appropriate headspace.

- **Seal and Process:**

  - Apply lids and process the jars in a boiling water bath or pressure canner, following specific guidelines for the type of plant being canned.

- **Cool and Store:**

  - Allow the jars to cool, ensuring a proper seal. Store in a cool, dark place.

4. Fermentation:

- **Clean and Prepare:**

  - Clean the wild edible plants and chop them into appropriate sizes for fermentation.

- **Brine Preparation:**

- Prepare a brine solution (salt and water) and ensure the salinity is suitable for fermentation.

- **Fermentation Vessel:**

  - Pack the chopped plants into a fermentation vessel, submerging them in the brine solution.

- **Fermentation Process:**

  - Allow the plants to ferment at the right temperature and duration, usually a few days to weeks, depending on the desired taste and texture.

- **Store Fermented Foods:**

  - Once the fermentation is complete, transfer the fermented plants to airtight containers and store them in the refrigerator.

5. Pickling:

- **Prepare Brine:**

  - Prepare a pickling brine using vinegar, water, salt, and desired spices.

- **Slice and Pack:**

  - Slice the wild edibles and pack them into sterilized jars, adding spices, garlic, or herbs for flavour.

- **Pour Brine and Seal:**

  - Pour the brine into the jars, ensuring the plants are completely covered. Seal the jars.

- **Refrigerate or Process:**

  - Refrigerate for quick pickles or process the jars in a boiling water bath for longer shelf life.

Preserving and fermenting wild edible plants allow you to enjoy their flavours and nutrition beyond their typical season. Experiment with different preservation methods and find what works best for the wild edibles you harvest. Always prioritize safety and follow established guidelines for preservation techniques.

Exploring Unique Foraging Environments

Foraging for wild edibles is an exciting way to connect with nature, learn about plants, and harvest fresh, natural foods. Exploring unique foraging environments adds an extra layer of adventure and discovery to this activity. Here is a guide to exploring various exceptional foraging environments:

1. Coastal Foraging:

- **Explore Shorelines:**

    - Visit coastlines to discover an abundance of seaweed, edible beach plants, coastal herbs, and sea vegetables.

- **Harvest Responsibly:**

- Follow guidelines to harvest seaweed sustainably, ensuring minimal impact on marine ecosystems.

- **Popular Edibles:**

  - Seaweeds like dulse, nori, kelp, and various coastal herbs and plants.

2. Forest Foraging:

- **Deep Forests:**

  - Venture into deep forests to forage for mushrooms, wild berries, nuts, and an array of forest floor plants.

- **Identify Trees:**

  - Learn to identify different tree species as they often host edible mushrooms and provide nuts or edible barks.

- **Popular Edibles:**

  - Morel and chanterelle mushrooms, blueberries, blackberries, acorns, and pine nuts.

3. Mountain Foraging:

- **Alpine Meadows:**
    - Explore alpine meadows for unique wildflowers, mountain berries, and edible herbs growing at higher altitudes.
- **Safety Precautions:**
    - Be mindful of the altitude and weather conditions. Dress appropriately and bring necessary gear.
- **Popular Edibles:**
    - Alpine strawberries, juniper berries, mountain sorrel, and various alpine herbs.

4. Desert Foraging:

- **Desert Exploration:**
    - Visit deserts to find cacti, succulents, and other plants specially adapted to arid environments.
- **Learn Plant Adaptations:**

- Understand the unique adaptations of desert plants that make them edible and valuable for survival.

- **Popular Edibles:**

  - Prickly pears, agave, mesquite beans, and desert edible greens.

5. Urban Foraging:

- **City Parks and Green Spaces:**

  - Explore parks, abandoned lots, and green areas within the city to discover edible plants and urban foraging opportunities.

- **Safety Considerations:**

  - Be aware of pollution and contamination risks in urban environments. Choose clean and safe locations for foraging.

- **Popular Edibles:**

  - Dandelions, plantains, mulberries, and various edible flowers.

6. Riverside Foraging:

- **Riverbanks and Creeks:**

    - Forage along riverbanks and creeks for water-loving plants, edible aquatic greens, and aquatic life.

- **Be Environmentally Conscious:**

    - Avoid disturbing aquatic habitats and be mindful of your impact on the ecosystem.

- **Popular Edibles:**

    - Watercress, wild leeks, cattails, and freshwater mussels.

7. Meadow and Grassland Foraging:

- **Explore Open Grasslands:**

    - Wander through meadows and grasslands to find an array of wildflowers, edible greens, and grass seeds.

- **Identify Edible Plants:**

- Learn to identify grasses, flowers, and herbs that are safe for consumption.

- **Popular Edibles:**

  - Clover, dandelion greens, plantain, and wild grass seeds.

Safety Tips for Exploring Unique Foraging Environments:

- Prioritize safety and always be aware of your surroundings.

- Carry necessary foraging tools, a first aid kit, and ample water and snacks.

- Familiarize yourself with local regulations and permissions for foraging.

- If uncertain about a plant's identification, do not consume it.

- Leave no trace and respect the environment you are exploring.

Exploring unique foraging environments is an adventure that allows you to connect with nature, broaden your plant knowledge, and savour a diverse array of wild edibles. Always ensure responsible foraging practices and respect the ecosystems you explore.

CHAPTER NINE
Nutrition and Culinary Uses

Nutritional Value of Wild Edible Plants: Nature's Bounty

Wild edible plants offer a diverse array of nutrients and can be valuable additions to a balanced diet. They often contain essential vitamins, minerals, antioxidants, and dietary fibre. Here is an overview of the nutritional value of common wild edible plants:

1. Leafy Greens:

- **Dandelion Greens:**

    - Rich in vitamins A, C, K, and folate.

    - High in calcium, iron, and antioxidants.

- **Lamb's Quarters:**

    - Excellent source of vitamins A, C, and K.

- High in calcium, iron, and protein.

- **Purslane:**

    - Abundant in vitamins A, C, E, and omega-3 fatty acids.

    - Contains calcium, iron, and potassium.

2. Berries:

- **Blueberries:**

    - Packed with antioxidants, particularly anthocyanins.

    - Good source of vitamins C and K, and dietary fibre.

- **Blackberries:**

    - High in vitamins C and K, and manganese.

    - Rich in dietary fibre and antioxidants.

- **Raspberries:**

    - Rich in vitamins C and K, and manganese.

    - High in dietary fibre and antioxidants.

3. Nuts and Seeds:

- **Acorns:**

    - Rich in healthy fats, protein, and fibre.

    - Good source of vitamins B6, folate, calcium, and iron.

- **Pine Nuts:**

    - High in healthy fats and protein.

    - Rich in vitamins E and K, and essential minerals like zinc and magnesium.

4. Roots and Tubers:

- **Wild Yam:**

    - Good source of dietary fiber, potassium, and manganese.

- **Burdock Root:**

    - Rich in dietary fibre, vitamin B6, folate, and potassium.

- **Wild Potatoes:**

    - High in carbohydrates, dietary fibre, and vitamin C.

5. Seaweed:

- **Nori:**

  - Rich in iodine, essential for thyroid function.

  - Good source of vitamins A, C, and B12, and minerals like iron and calcium.

- **Kelp:**

  - Abundant in iodine and essential minerals such as iron and calcium.

  - Contains vitamins A, C, and K.

6. Flowers:

- **Elderflowers:**

  - Rich in vitamins C and B6.

  - Contains antioxidants and anti-inflammatory properties.

- **Dandelion Flowers:**

  - Nutrient-rich, containing vitamins A and C.

7. Fruits:

- **Apples (Wild Varieties):**

  - Good source of dietary fibre, vitamins A and C.

  - Contains various antioxidants.

- **Mulberries:**

  - High in vitamins C and K, and iron.

  - Rich in dietary fibre and antioxidants.

Important Considerations:

- The nutritional content can vary based on the specific plant, growing conditions, and maturity at harvest.

- Wild edible plants often have a diverse nutrient profile, contributing to a well-rounded diet when consumed as part of a varied meal plan.

- Always ensure proper identification of wild plants and gather them from pollution-free areas to ensure safety and optimal nutritional value.

Wild edible plants, when appropriately identified and harvested, can significantly contribute to a nutritious diet by providing a variety of essential vitamins, minerals, and antioxidants. Incorporate them into your diet to enjoy the nutritional benefits nature has to offer.

Incorporating Wild Edibles into Your Diet

Incorporating wild edibles into your diet can be a rewarding and nutritious culinary adventure. However, it is essential to responsibly harvest, identify, and prepare these plants. Here is a guide on how to creatively and safely integrate wild edibles into your meals:

1. Education and Identification:

- **Thorough Research:**
  - Educate yourself about local wild edibles, their identification, seasons, and habitats.
- **Foraging Guides:**

- Utilize reliable foraging books, websites, or apps with clear images and descriptions for accurate identification.

- **Join Foraging Groups:**

  - Connect with local foraging groups or experts to learn from their experience and knowledge.

2. Responsible Harvesting:

- **Sustainable Practices:**

  - Harvest only what you need and avoid over-harvesting to ensure the continued growth and sustainability of wild plants.

- **Ethical Harvesting:**

  - Respect private property, protected areas, and wildlife habitats. Obtain necessary permissions for foraging.

3. Start Simple:

- **Familiarize with Flavours:**

- Begin by incorporating wild edibles with flavours similar to what you are accustomed to.

- **Mild Tasting Greens:**

  - Start with mild-tasting wild greens like dandelion leaves, lamb's quarters, or purslane in salads or sautés.

4. Wash and Prepare:

- **Thorough Cleaning:**

  - Wash wild edibles carefully to remove any dirt, insects, or debris.

- **Proper Preparation:**

  - Prepare them as you would other vegetables, ensuring they are cooked or processed appropriately for safety.

5. Experiment with Recipes:

- **Salads:**

  - Add a variety of wild edibles to your salads, mixing flavours and textures for a unique twist.

- **Smoothies:**

  - Incorporate wild berries, greens, or edible flowers into your morning smoothies for added nutrition and flavour.

- **Sauté or Stir-fry:**

  - Sauté wild greens with garlic, olive oil, and your favourite spices for a tasty side dish.

- **Infusions:**

  - Brew wild edible flowers or leaves to make refreshing teas or infusions.

6. Preserve for Future Use:

- **Drying:**

  - Dry wild edibles like herbs, flowers, or berries to use as seasonings or tea ingredients throughout the year.

- **Freezing:**

  - Freeze wild berries or greens for use in cooking or smoothies.

- **Pickling and Fermentation:**
  - Preserve wild edibles through pickling or fermentation for longer shelf life and unique flavours.

7. Blend with Common Ingredients:

- **Combine with Common Foods:**
  - Mix wild edibles with familiar ingredients to introduce them gradually into your meals.

- **Incorporate into Sauces:**
  - Blend wild herbs into sauces, pesto, or dips to enhance their flavour and nutritional content.

8. Experiment and Enjoy:

- **Be Creative:**
  - Experiment with wild edibles in various recipes to find combinations that suit your taste.

- **Enjoy the Journey:**

- Embrace the exploration and adventure that wild edibles bring to your culinary experiences.

Safety Precautions:

- **Proper Identification:** Be absolutely sure of the identification of any wild plant before consuming it.

- **Avoid Toxic Plants:** Familiarize yourself with poisonous plants and strictly avoid them.

- **Allergies:** Be cautious if you have allergies to certain plants or foods, even if they are wild edibles.

Incorporating wild edibles into your diet not only diversifies your meals but also reconnects you with nature and its offerings. With responsible harvesting and a creative approach to cooking, you can enjoy the unique flavours and nutritional benefits that wild edibles provide.

Creating Flavourful Recipes with Wild Plants

Cooking with wild plants allows you to infuse unique flavours and textures into your meals. Here's a guide to creating flavourful recipes using various wild plants:

1. Wild Green Salad:

- **Ingredients:**

    - Dandelion greens, lamb's quarters, purslane, wild lettuce, violets, or other wild greens.

    - Tomatoes, cucumbers, radishes, and any other desired salad vegetables.

    - Olive oil, lemon juice, salt, and pepper for dressing.

- **Directions:**

1. Wash and dry the wild greens and other salad vegetables.

2. Combine them in a bowl.

3.   Toss with olive oil, lemon juice, salt, and pepper for a refreshing salad.

2. Wild Berry Smoothie:

- **Ingredients:**

    - Wild berries (e.g., blackberries, raspberries, mulberries).

    - Greek yogurt or a dairy-free alternative.

    - Honey or maple syrup for sweetness.

    - Ice cubes (optional).

- **Directions:**

1.   Blend the wild berries, yogurt, and sweetener until smooth.

2.   Add ice cubes and blend again for a cool, delicious smoothie.

3. Stuffed Wild Grape Leaves:

- **Ingredients:**

    - Wild grape leaves (fresh or preserved).

- Rice cooked and seasoned.

- Ground lamb or lentils for a vegetarian option.

- Spices like mint, parsley, and dill.

- Olive oil, lemon juice, salt, and pepper.

- **Directions:**

1. Blanch the grape leaves and pat them dry.

2. Mix cooked rice, ground lamb or lentils, and spices to form a stuffing.

3. Roll the stuffing in grape leaves and cook with olive oil, lemon juice, salt, and pepper until tender.

4. Wild Herb Pesto:

- **Ingredients:**

  - Wild herbs (e.g., basil, wild garlic, dandelion leaves).

  - Pine nuts or walnuts.

- Garlic, olive oil, Parmesan cheese (optional), salt, and pepper.

- **Directions:**

1.   Blend the wild herbs, pine nuts, garlic, and olive oil until smooth.

2.   Stir in grated Parmesan cheese, salt, and pepper.

3.   Use the pesto as a pasta sauce, spread, or dip.

5. Nettle Soup:

- **Ingredients:**

  - Fresh nettle leaves.

  - Potatoes, onions, garlic, and vegetable broth.

  - Olive oil, salt, pepper, and cream or coconut milk (optional).

- **Directions:**

1.   Sauté onions and garlic in olive oil, then add chopped potatoes and nettles.

2.	Pour in vegetable broth and simmer until potatoes are tender.

3.	Blend the soup, season with salt and pepper, and add cream or coconut milk for creaminess.

6. Wild Flower Infused Tea:

- **Ingredients:**

    - Edible wild flowers (e.g., chamomile, elderflowers, lavender).

    - Hot water.

- **Directions:**

1.	Place a handful of edible flowers in a teapot or cup.

2.	Pour hot water over the flowers and steep for a few minutes.

3.	Strain and enjoy the aromatic and flavourful wild flower tea.

7. Wild Herb Frittata:

- **Ingredients:**

- Wild herbs (e.g., chickweed, sorrel, plantain).

- Eggs, bell peppers, onions, and cheese (optional).

- Olive oil, salt, and pepper.

- **Directions:**

1. Sauté chopped vegetables and wild herbs in olive oil until tender.

2. Pour beaten eggs over the mixture and cook until set.

3. Top with cheese, if desired, and season with salt and pepper.

Tips:

- **Experiment with Pairings:** Mix and match wild edibles to find unique flavour combinations that suit your taste.

- **Start Small:** Begin with small quantities of wild plants in your recipes and gradually adjust to your preference.

- **Record You're Creations:** Document your recipes, noting which wild plants you used and their flavours, to replicate successful dishes.

Wild edibles offer a diverse range of flavours and textures that can elevate your culinary experience. Be creative, embrace experimentation, and savour the delightful tastes that nature provides.

CHAPTER EIGHT
Popular Wild Edible Plant in us

Wild Greens and Herbs: A Bounty of Flavour and Nutrition

Wild greens and herbs, often abundant in various ecosystems, are a treasure trove of flavours and nutritional benefits. These plants, foraged directly from nature, add vibrancy and diversity to culinary creations. Here is a detailed guide on some common wild greens and herbs, along with ideas on how to use them:

1. Dandelion Greens (Taraxacum officinale):

- **Flavour:** Slightly bitter and peppery.

- **Preparation:** Use young leaves raw in salads or sauté with garlic and olive oil.

- **Health Benefits:** Rich in vitamins A, C, and K, as well as iron and calcium.

2. Stinging Nettle (Urtica dioica):

- **Flavour:** Earthy, slightly nutty, and similar to spinach.

- **Preparation:** Blanch to remove stinging hairs, then use in soups, stews, or as a substitute for spinach.

- **Health Benefits:** High in iron, vitamins, and minerals; known for anti-inflammatory properties.

3. Lamb's Quarters (Chenopodium album):

- **Flavour:** Similar to spinach but milder.

- **Preparation:** Enjoy raw in salads, sauté, or steam as a side dish.

- **Health Benefits:** Rich in vitamins A and C, calcium, and iron.

4. Chickweed (Stellaria media):

- **Flavour:** Mild, slightly grassy, with a hint of sweetness.

- **Preparation:** Add to salads, sandwiches, or blend into pesto.

- **Health Benefits:** Contains vitamins A, C, and D, as well as calcium and potassium.

5. Wild Garlic or Ramsons (Allium ursinum):

- **Flavour:** Intensely garlicky and pungent.

- **Preparation:** Use raw in salads, pesto, or cook in soups, stir-fries, or omelettes.

- **Health Benefits:** Contains vitamins A and C; known for its antibacterial properties.

6. Plantain (Plantago major):

- **Flavour:** Mild, slightly nutty or mushroom-like.

- **Preparation:** Enjoy young leaves raw in salads or sauté for a side dish.

- **Health Benefits:** High in vitamins A, C, and K, as well as calcium and fibre.

7. Wood Sorrel (Oxalis spp.):

- **Flavour:** Tangy, lemony, with a pleasant acidity.

- **Preparation:** Use raw in salads, as a garnish, or to make a refreshing tea.

- **Health Benefits:** Rich in vitamin C and antioxidants.

8. Wild Mint (Mentha spp.):

- **Flavour:** Refreshing, minty, and aromatic.

- **Preparation:** Use in teas, infuse into oils, or sprinkle over dishes for a burst of flavour.

- **Health Benefits:** Aids digestion and provides a soothing aroma.

9. Wild Thyme (Thymus serpyllum):

- **Flavour:** Strong, aromatic, slightly sweet, and earthy.

- **Preparation:** Use fresh or dried in soups, stews, marinades, or infuse into oils and vinegars.

- **Health Benefits:** Contains antioxidants and has antimicrobial properties.

10. Rosemary (Rosmarinus officinalis):

- **Flavour:** Strong, pine, and slightly peppery.

- **Preparation:** Use as a seasoning for roasted vegetables, meats, or in infusions.

- **Health Benefits:** Rich in antioxidants and has anti-inflammatory properties.

Culinary Ideas:

- **Wild Green Salad:** Mix a variety of wild greens with a simple vinaigrette, nuts, and cheese for a refreshing salad.

- **Herb-Infused Oil:** Infuse wild herbs like thyme, rosemary, or wild garlic into olive oil for a flavourful base in cooking.

- **Wild Herb Pesto:** Blend wild herbs with garlic, nuts, Parmesan cheese, and olive oil to make a tasty pesto for pasta, bread, or as a dip.

- **Wild Herb Butter:** Mix finely chopped wild herbs into softened butter, allowing the flavours to meld, and use as a spread or seasoning for dishes.

By incorporating these wild greens and herbs into your culinary repertoire, you can elevate your dishes, infusing them with unique flavours and reaping the health benefits these wild plants have to offer. Always ensure responsible foraging and verify the identification of wild plants before consumption.

Berries and Fruits: Nature's Sweet Bounty

Berries and fruits from the wild offer a burst of flavours, vibrant colours, and a nutritional profile that enriches any meal. From tangy berries to sweet fruits, they can be eaten fresh, incorporated into a variety of dishes, or preserved for future use. Here's a detailed guide on common wild berries and fruits, along with creative culinary uses:

1. Blueberries (Vaccinium spp.):

- **Flavour:** Sweet and mildly tangy.

- **Uses:** Eat fresh; add to pancakes, muffins, jams, or desserts.

- **Health Benefits:** Rich in antioxidants, vitamins C and K, and fibre.

2. Blackberries (Rubus fruticosus):

- **Flavour:** Sweet and slightly tart.

- **Uses:** Fresh consumption, jams, pies, cobblers, or infusions for beverages.

- **Health Benefits:** High in fibre, vitamin C, and antioxidants.

3. Raspberries (Rubus idaeus):

- **Flavour:** Sweet and slightly tangy.

- **Uses:** Fresh consumption, desserts, jams, sauces, or as garnish.

- **Health Benefits:** Rich in dietary fibre, vitamins C and K, and antioxidants.

4. Strawberries (Fragaria × ananassa):

- **Flavour:** Sweet and juicy.

- **Uses:** Fresh in salads, desserts, jams, smoothies, or dipped in chocolate.

- **Health Benefits:** High in vitamin C, manganese, and antioxidants.

5. Elderberries (Sambucus nigra):

- **Flavour:** Tart and earthy.

- **Uses:** Jams, syrups, pies, wines, teas, or medicinal infusions.

- **Health Benefits:** Immune-boosting properties and rich in vitamins and antioxidants.

6. Huckleberries (Vaccinium spp.):

- **Flavour:** Sweet, with a unique blend of tartness.

- **Uses:** Fresh consumption, jams, pies, muffins, or sauces.

- **Health Benefits:** High in vitamins C and K, fibre, and antioxidants.

7. Apples (Malus domestica):

- **Flavour:** Sweet and crisp.

- **Uses:** Fresh consumption, pies, crisps, sauces, or dried as chips.

- **Health Benefits:** Rich in fibre, vitamin C, and various antioxidants.

8. Pears (Pyrus):

- **Flavour:** Sweet and juicy.

- **Uses:** Fresh in salads, desserts, jams, or poached.

- **Health Benefits:** Good source of dietary fibre, vitamin C, and potassium.

9. Mulberries (Morus spp.):

- **Flavour:** Sweet and mildly tart.

- **Uses:** Fresh consumption, jams, pies, or dried for snacks.

- **Health Benefits:** High in vitamin C, iron, potassium, and dietary fibre.

10. Cherries (Prunus avium and Prunus cerasus):

- **Flavour:** Sweet to tart, depending on the variety.

- **Uses:** Fresh in salads, desserts, jams, or as a topping.

- **Health Benefits:** Rich in vitamins A and C, antioxidants, and anti-inflammatory compounds.

Culinary Ideas:

- **Berry Compote:** Cook mixed berries with a bit of sugar to make a compote for topping pancakes, ice cream, or yogurt.

- **Fruit Salad:** Combine a variety of fresh fruits for a refreshing and colourful fruit salad, garnished with mint leaves.

- **Wild Berry Jam:** Use wild berries to prepare delicious jams, perfect for spreading on toast or filling pastries.

- **Fruit Smoothies:** Blend a mix of fruits with yogurt or juice to create tasty and nutritious smoothies.

With these delicious wild berries and fruits, you can explore an array of culinary delights, infusing your meals with nature's sweetness and an abundance of health benefits. Always ensure responsible foraging and verify the identification of wild berries and fruits before consumption.

Nuts and Seeds: Nature's Nutritional Powerhouses

Nuts and seeds are not only delicious and versatile in culinary applications, but they also offer a rich source of essential nutrients, healthy fats, protein, and fibre. Whether consumed raw, roasted, or ground into various products, nuts and seeds add both flavour and nutritional value to a wide array of dishes. Here is a comprehensive guide on common wild nuts and seeds and how to use them:

1. Acorns (Quercus spp.):

- **Flavour:** Mildly nutty with a slightly sweet taste.

- **Preparation:** Process acorns to remove tannins, then grind into flour or roast for consumption.

- **Uses:** Acorn flour for baking, soups, or as a coffee substitute.

- **Nutritional Benefits:** Rich in carbohydrates, fibre, and healthy fats.

2. Pine Nuts (Pinus spp.)

- **Flavour:** Sweet and nutty.

- **Preparation:** Extract pine nuts from pinecones and use raw or lightly toasted.

- **Uses:** In salads, pesto, desserts, or as a garnish.

- **Nutritional Benefits:** Good source of healthy fats, protein, and iron.

3. Hazelnuts (Corylus avellana)

- **Flavour:** Rich, slightly sweet, and nutty.

- **Preparation:** Roast hazelnuts to enhance flavour and remove the skins, then use completely or ground.

- **Uses:** In baking, spreads (e.g., Nutella), desserts, or salads.

- **Nutritional Benefits:** High in protein, healthy fats, vitamin E, and folate.

4. Walnuts (Juglans regia):

- **Flavour:** Mildly bitter, rich, and earthy.

- **Preparation:** Use raw or toasted to enhance flavour.

- **Uses:** In salads, baking, granola, or as a topping.

- **Nutritional Benefits:** High in omega-3 fatty acids, protein, and antioxidants.

5. Sunflower Seeds (Helianthus annuus):

- **Flavour:** Nutty and slightly sweet.

- **Preparation:** Roast sunflower seeds with a bit of salt for enhanced taste and crunch.

- **Uses:** Snacking, salads, granola, trail mix, or garnish.

- **Nutritional Benefits:** Excellent source of vitamin E, magnesium, and selenium.

6. Pumpkin Seeds (Cucurbita pepo):

- **Flavour:** Nutty with a slightly sweet and earthy taste.

- **Preparation:** Roast pumpkin seeds with spices or salt for added flavour.

- **Uses:** Snacking, salads, baking, or as a topping.

- **Nutritional Benefits:** High in protein, iron, magnesium, and zinc.

7. Sesame Seeds (Sesamum indicum):

- **Flavour:** Nutty and slightly earthy.

- **Preparation:** Toast sesame seeds to deepen the flavour.

- **Uses:** In baking, cooking, sauces (e.g., tahini), or as a topping.

- **Nutritional Benefits:** Rich in healthy fats, protein, calcium, and iron.

8. Chia Seeds (Salvia hispanica):

- **Flavour:** Mild, slightly nutty.

- **Preparation:** Soak chia seeds to form a gel-like texture.

- **Uses:** Smoothies, puddings, baked goods, or as a thickener.

- **Nutritional Benefits:** High in fibre, omega-3 fatty acids, and antioxidants.

Culinary Ideas:

- **Nut Butters:** Blend nuts like hazelnuts, almonds, or peanuts to make delicious and creamy nut butters for spreads or dips.

- **Trail Mix:** Mix a variety of nuts and seeds with dried fruits for a portable and energizing snack.

- **Granola:** Incorporate a mixture of nuts and seeds into homemade granola for a crunchy and nutritious breakfast option.

- **Baking:** Use nuts and seeds in baked goods like bread, muffins, cookies, or cakes for added texture and flavour.

Nuts and seeds, whether consumed as a snack, a topping, or an ingredient in various dishes, provide an array of flavours and nutritional benefits. Enjoy their versatility in your culinary adventures while reaping the health advantages they offer. Always ensure responsible foraging and verify the identification of wild nuts and seeds before consumption.

Roots and Tubers: Earthy Delights from Beneath the Surface

Roots and tubers, often hidden beneath the soil, are nutrient-dense, starchy vegetables that have been a crucial part of human diets for centuries. They offer a rich source of carbohydrates, fibre, vitamins, and minerals. Here is a detailed guide on common wild roots and tubers and how to use them:

1. Wild Carrots (Daucus carota):

- **Flavour:** Sweet, earthy, and slightly peppery.

- **Preparation:** Wash and peel, then consume raw, roasted, or boiled.

- **Uses:** Salads, stir-fries, soups, or as a side dish.

- **Nutritional Benefits:** Rich in beta-carotene, fibre, vitamins, and minerals.

2. Wild Radishes (Raphanus raphanistrum):

- **Flavour:** Peppery and slightly spicy.

- **Preparation:** Wash, peel, and slice for raw consumption or sautéing.

- **Uses:** Salads, stir-fries, pickles, or garnish.

- **Nutritional Benefits:** Good source of fibre, vitamins, and minerals.

3. Wild Yam (Dioscorea spp.):

- **Flavour:** Mild, starchy, and slightly sweet.

- **Preparation:** Peel and cook thoroughly by boiling, baking, or steaming.

- **Uses:** Soups, stews, mashed, or used as a base for various dishes.

- **Nutritional Benefits:** High in carbohydrates, fibre, and some vitamins.

4. Burdock Root (Arctium lappa):

- **Flavour:** Mild, slightly sweet, and earthy.

- **Preparation:** Scrub, peel, and cook by boiling or sautéing.

- **Uses:** Stir-fries, soups, stews, or pickled.

- **Nutritional Benefits:** Good source of dietary fibre, vitamins, and minerals.

5. Wild Potatoes (Solanum spp.):

- **Flavour:** Mild, starchy, and slightly nutty.

- **Preparation:** Wash, peel, and cook by boiling, baking, or frying.

- **Uses:** Mash, roast, fry, or incorporate into stews and soups.

- **Nutritional Benefits:** Rich in carbohydrates, fibre, vitamins, and minerals.

Culinary Ideas:

- **Root Vegetable Medley:** Roast a variety of roots like carrots, radishes, and wild potatoes with olive oil, herbs, and seasoning for a flavourful medley.

- **Mashed Roots:** Boil and mash roots like wild yam, carrots, or burdock for a delicious side dish, seasoned to taste.

- **Root Soups:** Combine various roots in a hearty soup with broth, vegetables, and spices for a nutritious meal.

- **Stir-Fried Roots:** Sauté a mixture of roots with your favourite vegetables, seasoning, and a splash of soy sauce for a tasty stir-fry.

Roots and tubers provide an earthy and hearty addition to your culinary repertoire. Enjoy their diverse flavours and nutritional benefits in a variety of dishes, ranging from side dishes to soups and beyond. Always ensure responsible foraging and verify the identification of wild roots and tubers before consumption.

Conclusion,

Wild edible plant foraging is a multifaceted activity that encompasses both ecological and cultural dimensions. The practice involves the identification, harvesting, and consumption of various plant species found in natural environments. Throughout history, humans have relied on wild edible plants for sustenance and nutrition, demonstrating a deep-rooted relationship with the natural world and its resources.

Engaging in wild edible plant foraging offers several benefits. Firstly, it fosters a stronger connection between individuals and their surroundings, encouraging a deeper appreciation for nature and its diverse flora. Learning to identify and utilize wild edible plants promotes environmental awareness and conservation efforts, as foragers develop an understanding of ecosystems and sustainable harvesting practices.

Additionally, wild edible plant foraging can contribute to a more sustainable and diversified diet. Wild plants often offer unique flavours, textures, and nutrients that may not be readily available in commercial produce. Incorporating wild edibles into one's diet can enhance nutritional variety and potentially contribute to a more resilient food system.

However, responsible foraging is paramount to ensure the preservation of ecosystems and the continuation of this ancient practice. Sustainable harvesting practices, such as taking only a portion of a plant to allow for regrowth, respecting regulations and conservation areas, and avoiding rare or endangered species, are essential to maintain the delicate balance of natural environments.

It is crucial for individuals interested in wild edible plant foraging to educate themselves thoroughly. This education should cover plant identification, including distinguishing between edible and poisonous species, understanding seasonal availability, and appreciating the importance of sustainable foraging practices. Formal training, field guides, and mentorship from experienced foragers can be invaluable resources in acquiring the necessary knowledge and skills.

In conclusion, wild edible plant foraging holds great potential for promoting a harmonious relationship between humans and the natural world. When approached responsibly and sustainably, it can contribute to a deeper understanding of ecosystems, dietary diversity, and the preservation of valuable plant resources for future generations.